Essential Duas for Muslims
(Shafi'i Madhhab)

Title: Essential Duas for Muslims (Shafi'i Madhhab)

Prepared by:
Jamiatul Ulama (KZN) for Madrasah Imdaadiyya
Ta'limi Board
4 Third Avenue
P.O.Box 26024
Isipingo Beach
4115
South Africa

Tel: (+27) 31 912 2172
Fax: (+27) 31 902 9268
E-mail: info@talimiboardkzn.org
Website: www.talimiboardkzn.org

First edition: July   2019

Published by:
Islamic Book Store
302 Saad Residancy
M G Road
Bardoli
Gujarat India
394601

Table of Contents	Page	Tick
Grade One		
1. 1st Kalima	1	
2. 2nd Kalima	2	
3. 3rd Kalima	3	
4. 4th Kalima	4	
5. 5th Kalima	5	
6. Imaani Mujmal	7	
7. Imaani Mufassal	8	
8. Greeting a Muslim	9	
9. Reply to a greeting	10	
10. Welcoming someone	10	
11. Before Eating	11	
12. Forget to read the dua	11	
13. After Eating	12	
14. Before Sleeping (1)	13	
15. When Awakening	13	
16. Before toilet	14	
17. After toilet	15	
18. When thanking someone	16	
19. Intending to do something	16	
20. Sneezing	17	
21. Increase in knowledge	18	
22. Dua for parents	18	
23. Durood Shareef	19	
Grade Two		
24. Takbeer	21	
25. Dua-ul-Istiftaah	21	
26. Ta'awwuz	22	
27. Tasmiya	22	
28. Tasbeeh in ruku	22	
29. Tasmee'	23	
30. Dua in Qaumah (1)	23	
31. Dua in Qaumah (2)	24	
32. Tasbeeh in Sajda	24	
33. Dua in Jalsa	25	
34. Tashah'hud	26	
35. Durood-e-Ibraheem	27	
36. After Durood-e-Ibraheem	28	
37. Azaan	29	
38. Iqaamah	30	

Table of Contents	Page	Tick
39. Dua after Azaan	32	
Grade Three		
40. Before Wudhu	35	
41. Whilst making Wudhu	35	
42. After Wudhu	36	
43. Entering the Masjid	37	
44. Leaving the Masjid	37	
45. After drinking water	38	
46. After drinking milk	39	
47. When wearing clothes	39	
48. Looking into the mirror	40	
49. Entering the home	41	
50. When leaving home	42	
51. When bidding farewell	43	
52. When it rains	43	
53. On hearing good news	44	
54. When a loss occurs	44	
55. When in bodily pain	45	
56. When in difficulty	45	
57. Dua for death on Imaan	46	
Grade Four		
58. Getting into a vehicle	48	
59. When the vehicle moves	49	
60. Returning from journey	49	
61. Entering a town or city	50	
62. Dua-e-Qunoot	51	
63. Dua after witr	52	
64. On seeing the new moon	53	
65. Dua for fasting	54	
66. When breaking fast	55	
67. Eating elsewhere (1)	56	
68. Eating elsewhere (2)	57	
69. Eating 1st fruit season	58	
70. Afflicted with a calamity	59	
Grade Five		
71. When in financial difficulty	61	
72. Seeing someone in distress	62	
73. Dua for fever	63	
74. Visiting the sick	64	
75. At the time of death	65	

Table of Contents	Page	Tick
76. After 2nd Takbeer in Janazah Salaah	66	
77. After 3rd Takbeer in Janazah Salaah	67	
78. After 4th Takbeer in Janazah Salaah	68	
79. Entering the graveyard	68	
80. Dua to be recited in graveyard	69	
81. Laying the dead in the grave	70	
82. Filling the grave with soil	71	
Grade Six		
83. At the time of sunset	73	
84. When seeing the moon	73	
85. At the time of drought	74	
86. Excessive rain	74	

Table of Contents	Page	Tick
87. Wearing new clothes	75	
88. Leaving a gathering	76	
89. Entering a shopping centre	77	
90. 99 Names of Allah Ta'ala	79	
Grade Seven		
91. Laying the animal down	82	
92. When slaughtering	84	
93. Sayyidul Istighfaar	85	
94. Istikharah dua	87	
Alternative Istikharah Dua	89	
95. Most Comprehensive Dua	90	

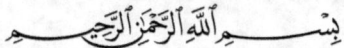

All praise is due to Allah Ta'ala, The Supreme Master of all the worlds. Countless Durood and Salaam be upon our beloved Nabi, Sayyidina Muhammad ﷺ.

We have been taught by Rasulullah ﷺ to recite duas at different occasions of our life. From the time we awaken till the time we go to sleep we have been taught to recite these duas. In this manner our entire day passes in the remembrance of Allah Ta'ala. It is mentioned in the Hadith that Rasulullah ﷺ used to remember Allah Ta'ala at all times. A great amount of the constant remembrance was by means of the recitation of the duas for the various occasions. The recitation of these duas also strengthens our bond with Allah Ta'ala and increases the love for our Creator in our hearts.

The Noble Sahaabah (companions) of Rasulullah ﷺ preserved these duas and in turn taught it to the Ummah.

Al-hamdulillah, it is only with the *fadhal* of Allah Ta'ala that the Ta'limi Board (KZN) has compiled these duas in a booklet for the easy reference for children in the makaatib. The duas have been separated in grades to facilitate easier learning for them.

An effort to mention some virtues of each dua was also made to serve as an encouragement for the pupils to recite these duas.

Parents need to play an important role of constantly encouraging and reminding their children to recite these duas at the appropriate time. Thus when the child is woken up in the morning, before he enters the toilet and after he leaves, before and after eating and at all other occasions, the parents should remind the child to recite the dua. In this way it will become a part of their lives and the purpose of teaching these duas will be achieved, insha Allah.

We make dua to Allah Ta'ala to accept this publication and make it a means of *hidaayat* for the *ummah* as well as *Sadaqah-e-Jaariyah* for us all. Aameen.

Ta'limi Board (KwaZulu Natal)

GRADE 1

1. Kalimah Tayyibah

لَا اِلٰهَ اِلَّا اللهُ مُحَمَّدٌ رَسُوْلُ اللهِ

There is no God besides Allah Ta'ala. Hadhrat Muhammad ﷺ is the messenger of Allah Ta'ala.

VIRTUE:

Hadhrat Abu Darda رضي الله عنه reports that Nabi ﷺ said, "Whoever reads this kalimah 100 times daily, his face will shine like a full moon on the Day of Qiyaamah."

(Fazail-e-A'amaal, Zikr pg.156 from Tabraani)

GRADE 1

2. Kalimah Shahaadah

اَشْهَدُ اَنْ لَّا اِلٰهَ اِلَّا اللهُ وَاَشْهَدُ اَنَّ مُحَمَّدًا عَبْدُهٗ وَرَسُوْلُهٗ

I bear witness that there is no God besides Allah Ta'ala and I bear witness that Hadhrat Muhammad ﷺ is His servant and messenger.

Virtue

Nabi ﷺ said that on the day of Qiyaamah, in the presence of all mankind, Allah Ta'ala will call a person from my Ummah, who will have ninety-nine registers of bad deeds and each register will be as long as one can see. Then Allah Ta'ala will say there is one good deed to your credit. A small piece of paper with this Kalimah will be given to him. The ninety-nine registers will be placed on one side of the scale and this kalimah will be placed on the other side. The kalimah will outweigh the ninety-nine registers.

GRADE 1

3. Kalimah Tamjid

سُبْحَانَ اللهِ وَالْحَمْدُ لِلّهِ وَلَا اِلٰهَ اِلَّا اللهُ وَاللهُ اَكْبَرُ وَلَا حَوْلَ وَلَا قُوَّةَ اِلَّا بِاللهِ الْعَلِيِّ الْعَظِيْمِ

Glory be to Allah Ta'ala and all praise be to Allah Ta'ala. There is no God besides Allah Ta'ala. And, Allah Ta'ala is the Greatest. There is no power and might except from Allah Ta'ala, The Most High, The Great.

Virtue

One who recites this kalimah 100 times in the morning and 100 times in the evening gets the reward of 100 Haj, giving 100 horses in the path of Allah, freeing 100 slaves,…and no one can match your sawaab for that day, unless he/she did the same.

(Tirmizi #3471)

4. Kalimah Tawheed

لَا اِلٰهَ اِلَّا اللهُ وَحْدَهُ لَا شَرِيكَ لَهُ لَهُ الْمُلْكُ وَلَهُ الْحَمْدُ يُحْيِي وَيُمِيتُ بِيَدِهِ الْخَيْرُ وَهُوَ عَلَىٰ كُلِّ شَيْءٍ قَدِيرٌ

There is no God besides Allah Ta'ala. He is One. He has no partner. For Him is the kingdom and for Him is all praise. He gives life and causes death. In His hand is all good. And He has power over everything.

Virtue

One who recites this kalimah 10 times after Maghrib Salaah, will be greatly rewarded and Allah Ta'ala will send special guardian angels to protect him from shaytaan right until the morning.

(Tirmizi 3474 and 3534)

5. Kalimah Rad-de Kufr

اَللّٰهُمَّ اِنِّى اَعُوْذُ بِكَ مِنْ اَنْ اُشْرِكَ بِكَ شَيْئًا وَّاَنَا اَعْلَمُ بِهٖ وَاَسْتَغْفِرُكَ لِمَا لَا اَعْلَمُ بِهٖ تُبْتُ عَنْهُ وَتَبَرَّاْتُ مِنَ الْكُفْرِ وَالشِّرْكِ وَالْمَعَاصِىْ كُلِّهَا اَسْلَمْتُ وَاٰمَنْتُ وَاَقُوْلُ لَا اِلٰهَ اِلَّا اللهُ مُحَمَّدٌ رَسُوْلُ اللهِ

GRADE 1

O Allah Ta'ala! I seek protection in You from that I should join any partner with You knowingly. I seek Your forgiveness from that which I do not know. I repent from ignorance. I free myself from disbelief and from joining partners with You, and I free myself from all sins. I submit to Your will. I believe and I declare: There is no God besides **Allah Ta'ala** Hadhrat Muhammad ﷺ is the **Messenger of Allah Ta'ala**.

Virtue

Nabi ﷺ once said that, "Evil and Shirk can enter the heart." The Sahaabah رضي الله عنهم were worried when they heard this. Nabi ﷺ then said, "Beware of Shirk, for it is quieter than the crawling of an ant." Then Nabi ﷺ asked, "Must I teach you something that will save you from all forms of Shir'k, the minor and the major?" He then taught them to read the 5th kalima.

(Ibnus Sunni pg. 250)

GRADE 1

6. Imaani-Mujmal

$$\text{اَمَنْتُ بِاللهِ كَمَا هُوَ بِاَسْمَآئِهٖ وَصِفَاتِهٖ وَقَبِلْتُ جَمِيْعَ اَحْكَامِهٖ}$$

I believe in Allah Ta'ala as He is by His names and His qualities and I accept all His orders.

Virtue

Nabi ﷺ explained that at times Shaytaan tries to confuse a person regarding his belief in Allah Ta'ala, and he (Shaytaan) should just be ignored. (Mishkaat pg.18) This kalimah is very effective in repelling doubts and confusion from Shaytaan.

7. Imaani-Mufassal

$$\text{اٰمَنْتُ بِاللهِ وَمَلٰٓئِكَتِهٖ وَكُتُبِهٖ وَرُسُلِهٖ وَالْيَوْمِ الْاٰخِرِ وَالْقَدْرِ خَيْرِهٖ وَشَرِّهٖ مِنَ اللهِ تَعَالٰى وَالْبَعْثِ بَعْدَ الْمَوْتِ}$$

I believe in Allah Ta'ala, His Angels, His Books, His Messengers, the Last Day, and in Taqdeer, that all good and bad is from Allah Ta'ala, and I believe in the life after death.

Note:

Once Nabi ﷺ was asked what is Imaan? Nabi ﷺ explained the important aspects which one has to believe in, in order to be a Believer.

(Bukhaari V.1 Pg. 12)

These are all mentioned in Imaan-e-Mufassal.

GRADE 1

Note:

Reading of all seven kalimahs every night is a type of renewal of our Imaan in our beliefs, which we need to do especially after being exposed to many un Islamic beliefs in schools, newspapers, etc. Caution demands that a person renews his Imaan everyday.

8. When greeting a Muslim, say

اَلسَّلَامُ عَلَيْكُمْ وَ رَحْمَةُ اللهِ وَ بَرَكَا تُهُ

May the Peace, Mercy and blessings of Allah Ta'ala be upon you.

GRADE 1

9. In reply to a greeting, say

$$\text{وَ عَلَيْكُمُ السَّلَامُ وَ رَحْمَةُ اللهِ وَ بَرَكَاتُهُ}$$

May the Peace, Mercy and blessings of Allah Ta'ala be upon you.

10. When welcoming someone say

$$\text{اَهْلًا وَ سَهْلًا وَ مَرْحَبًا}$$

(May you enter and) be as one of us, be at ease and comfortable, and welcome (to you).

(Tirmizi, Ibnu Majah)

GRADE 1

11. Before eating

بِسْمِ اللهِ وَعَلٰى بَرَكَةِ اللهِ

In the name of Allah Ta'ala and upon the blessings of Allah Ta'ala.

(Al-Hisnul Haseen Pg. 141)

Virtue

One who reads this dua will receive blessing in one's meals.

12. When forgetting to recite the dua before eating

بِسْمِ اللهِ اَوَّلَهُ وَ اٰخِرَهُ

In the name of Allah Ta'ala in the beginning and the end.

(Abu Dawood, Vol. 2, Pg. 173)

Virtue

Once Rasulullah ﷺ saw a man who started his meal without saying بِسْمِ اللهِ. When he was about to finish, he remembered and recited بِسْمِ اللهِ اَوَّلَهُ وَ اٰخِرَهُ. Rasulullah ﷺ said: From the begining of the meal, Shaytaan was eating with him, but when he remembered and read this dua, Shaytaan couldn't join any more, instead whatever Shaytaan ate, he had to vomit it out.

13. After eating

$$\text{اَلْحَمْدُ لِلّٰهِ الَّذِىْ اَطْعَمَنَا وَسَقَانَا وَجَعَلَنَا مِنَ الْمُسْلِمِيْنَ}$$

All praise be to Allah Ta'ala who gave us food and drink and made us Muslims.

(Amalul yaumi wal laylah of Suyuti Page 32)

Virtue
Allah Ta'ala becomes pleased when His slave praises Him after meals.

Sunnats of eating
1. Wash both your hands before eating
2. Recite *'Bismillah wa'la barakatillah'* aloud.
3. Eat with the right hand.
4. Do not lean and eat.
5. Do not find fault with the food.
6. Whilst eating one should not remain completely silent.
7. Eat with three fingers as far as possible.
8. First remove the food from the dastarkhaan then get up.
9. After meals wash both your hands.

14. Before sleeping

$$\text{اَللّٰهُمَّ بِاسْمِكَ اَمُوْتُ وَاَحْيٰى}$$

O Allah Ta'ala, with Your name do I die and live.

(Tirmizi, Vol. 2, Pg. 178)

15. When awakening

$$\text{اَلْحَمْدُ لِلّٰهِ الَّذِىْ اَحْيَانَا بَعْدَ مَا اَمَاتَنَا وَاِلَيْهِ النُّشُوْرُ}$$

All praise is due to Allah Ta'ala who has given us life after death and to Him is our return after death.

(Bukhaari Vol. 2 Pg. 934)

Sunnats of sleeping

1. To sleep in the state of wudhu.
2. Dust the bed thrice before retiring to bed.
3. To apply surmah in both the eyes.
4. To brush the teeth with a miswaak.
5. To sleep on the right hand side.
6. To sleep with the right palm under the right cheek
7. To keep the knees slightly bent when sleeping.
8. To refrain from sleeping on one's stomach.
9. To sleep on a bed or to sleep on the floor are both sunnah.
10. To face the *Qiblah*.
11. To recite Aayatul Kursi before sleeping.
12. To recite Tasbeeh-e-Faathimi before sleeping.

16. Before entering the toilet

اَللّٰهُمَّ اِنِّيْ اَعُوْذُبِكَ مِنَ الْخُبُثِ وَالْخَبَائِثِ

O Allah Ta'ala, I seek Your protection from the male and female Devil.

(Tirmizi, Vol. 1, Pg. 3)

17. After leaving the toilet

$$\text{غُفْرَانَكَ اَلْحَمْدُ لِلّٰهِ الَّذِىْ اَذْهَبَ عَنِّى الْاَذٰى وَعَافَانِىْ}$$

O Allah! I seek Your forgiveness. All praise be to Allah Ta'ala who removed from me discomfort and gave me relief.

(Ibnu Majah, Pg.26)

Sunnats of the toilet

1. Enter the toilet with your head covered.
2. Enter the toilet with shoes.
3. Enter with the left foot.
4. Sit and urinate. One should never urinate whilst standing.
5. Leave the toilet with the right foot.
6. Recite the dua after coming out of the toilet.
7. Do not face or show one's back towards the Qiblah.
8. Be very careful of the splashes of urine. (Being unmindful in this regard causes one to be punished in the grave.)
9. After relieving oneself, to clean oneself with water.

GRADE 1

18. When thanking someone

جَزَاكَ اللهُ خَيْرًا

May Allah Ta'ala reward you well.

(Tirmizi Vol. 2, Pg. 24)

19. when intending to do something

اِنْ شَاءَ اللهُ

If Allah Ta'ala wills.

20. When Sneezing

$$\text{اَلْحَمْدُ لِلّٰهِ}$$

All praise be to Allah Ta'ala.

The listener's reply

$$\text{يَرْحَمُكَ اللّٰهُ}$$

May Allah Ta'ala have mercy on you.

The sneezer's response

$$\text{يَهْدِيْكُمُ اللّٰهُ وَ يُصْلِحُ بَالَكُمْ}$$

May Allah Ta'ala guide you and rectify your condition.

(Abu Dawood, Vol. 2, Pg. 338)

GRADE 1

21. For increase in knowledge

رَبِّ زِدْنِيْ عِلْمًا

O My Rabb, Increase me in knowledge.

(Sura Taaha, S.20/V.114)

Virtue

By reciting this Dua one's memory will strengthen Insha Allah.

22. Dua for parents

رَبِّ ارْحَمْهُمَا كَمَا رَبَّيَانِيْ صَغِيْرًا

O Allah Ta'ala! Have mercy upon them as they had mercy upon me when I was small.

(Surah. 17, V. 24)

Note:

1. Don't cause harm to your parents.
2. Don't speak rudely to them.
3. Don't back chat them.
4. Respect your grandparents like how you will respect your parents.
5. Make dua for them regularly.
6. Meet their friends and relatives in a good and friendly way.
7. If they have passed away, make dua for them and send e-saale thawab for them every day.

23. Durood Shareef

$$\text{اَللّٰهُمَّ صَلِّ عَلٰى سَيِّدِنَا مُحَمَّدٍ وَّعَلٰى اٰلِ سَيِّدِنَا مُحَمَّدٍ وَّبَارِكْ وَسَلِّمْ}$$

O Allah, grant Your special mercy on our Master Muhammad ﷺ and on the family of our Master Muhammad ﷺ and bless our Master Muhammad ﷺ and peace be on our Master Muhammad ﷺ.

Virtue:

1. One who recites Durood once will receive ten rewards, ten sins will be forgiven and his rank will be raised ten times in the hereafter.
2. Nabi ﷺ has said: "The closest person to me on the day of Qiyaamah is he who reads the most durood upon me."

24. Takbeer

اَللّٰهُ اَكْبَرُ

Allah Ta'ala is the greatest.

25. Dua-ul-Istiftaah

وَجَّهْتُ وَجْهِيَ لِلَّذِيْ فَطَرَ السَّمٰوٰتِ وَالْاَرْضَ حَنِيْفًا مُّسْلِمًا وَّ مَآ اَنَا مِنَ الْمُشْرِكِيْنَ اِنَّ صَلَاتِيْ وَ نُسُكِيْ وَ مَحْيَايَ وَ مَمَاتِيْ لِلّٰهِ رَبِّ الْعَالَمِيْنَ لَا شَرِيْكَ لَهُ وَ بِذَالِكَ اُمِرْتُ وَ اَنَا مِنَ الْمُسْلِمِيْنَ

I have firmly turned myself towards that Being Who has created the heavens and the earth, and I am not among the Mushrikeen. Verily, my Salaah, my sacrifice, my life and my death are for Allah Ta'ala, Rabb of the worlds. He has no partner, with this I have been commanded and I am the first of those who surrender.

26. Ta'awwuz

اَعُوْذُ بِاللّٰهِ مِنَ الشَّيْطَانِ الرَّجِيْمِ

I seek protection in Allah Ta'ala from shaytaan, the rejected.

27. Tasmiyah

بِسْمِ اللّٰهِ الرَّحْمٰنِ الرَّحِيْمِ

In the name of Allah Ta'ala, the Most Kind, the Most Merciful.

28. Dua in Ruku

سُبْحَانَ رَبِّيَ الْعَظِيْمِ وَ بِحَمْدِهْ

Glory be to My Rabb, the Great and all praise be to Him.

29. Tasmee'

سَمِعَ اللهُ لِمَنْ حَمِدَهْ

Allah Ta'ala hears the one who praises Him.

30. Dua in Qaumah (1)

اَللّٰهُمَّ رَبَّنَا وَ لَكَ الْحَمْدُ

O Allah Ta'ala! Our Sustainer! Unto You belongs all praise.

(Ibnu Majah, Pg. 62)

31. Dua in Qaumah (2)

رَبَّنَا وَلَكَ الْحَمْدُ حَمْدًا كَثِيرًا طَيِّبًا مُّبَارَكًا فِيهِ

O Allah Ta'ala, praise be to You many pure blessed praises.

(Bukhaari Vol.1 Pg.110)

Once, Nabi ﷺ was performing Salaah with the Sahaabah رضي الله عنهم when one Sahaabi read these words after standing up from ruku. When Rasulullah ﷺ completed the salaah, he asked who had read these words. One Sahaabi replied that he had recited it. Nabi ﷺ then said, "I saw 30 angels rushing to the words to see who would be the first to record them."

(Bukhaari Vol.1 Pg.110)

32. Tasbeeh in Sajdah

سُبْحَانَ رَبِّيَ الْأَعْلٰى وَ بِحَمْدِهْ

Glory be to My Rabb, the Most High, and all praise be to Him.

33. Dua in Jalsa

رَبِّ اغْفِرْ لِيْ وَارْحَمْنِيْ وَاجْبُرْنِيْ وَارْفَعْنِيْ وَارْزُقْنِيْ وَاهْدِنِيْ وَعَافِنِيْ وَاعْفُ عَنِّيْ

O my Rabb, forgive me, have mercy on me, compensate my loss, elevate me, provide me with sustenance and guide me, grant me peace and security and pardon me.

34. Tashah'hud

اَلتَّحِيَّاتُ الْمُبَارَكَاتُ الصَّلَوٰتُ الطَّيِّبَاتُ لِلّٰهِ اَلسَّلَامُ عَلَيْكَ اَيُّهَا النَّبِيُّ وَرَحْمَةُ اللهِ وَبَرَكَاتُهُ اَلسَّلَامُ عَلَيْنَا وَعَلٰى عِبَادِ اللهِ الصَّالِحِيْنَ اَشْهَدُ اَنْ لَّآ اِلٰهَ اِلَّا اللهُ وَاَشْهَدُ اَنَّ مُحَمَّدًا رَسُوْلُ اللهِ

All devotions offered through words, bodily actions and wealth are due to Allah Ta'ala. Peace be upon you, O Prophet ﷺ and the mercy of Allah Ta'ala and His blessings. Peace be upon us and on the pious (righteous) servants of Allah Ta'ala. I bear witness that there is no Deity besides Allah Ta'ala, and I bear witness that Muhammad ﷺ is the messenger of Allah.

35. Durood-e-Ibraaheem

اَللّٰهُمَّ صَلِّ عَلٰى سَيِّدِنَا مُحَمَّدٍ وَّعَلٰى اٰلِ مُحَمَّدٍ كَمَا صَلَّيْتَ عَلٰى اِبْرَاهِيْمَ وَعَلٰى اٰلِ اِبْرَاهِيْمَ وَبَارِكْ عَلٰى مُحَمَّدٍ وَعَلٰى اٰلِ مُحَمَّدٍ كَمَا بَارَكْتَ عَلٰى اِبْرَاهِيْمَ وَعَلٰى اٰلِ اِبْرَاهِيْمَ فِى الْعَالَمِيْنَ اِنَّكَ حَمِيْدٌ مَّجِيْدٌ

O Allah Ta'ala! Shower Your mercy on Muhammad ﷺ and his family (followers) as You showered Your mercy on Ibraaheem عَلَيْهِ السَّلَام and his family (followers).

And bless Muhammad ﷺ and his family (followers) as You have blessed Ibraaheem عَلَيْهِ السَّلَام and his family (followers) in the worlds. Surely You are Praiseworthy and Most High.

36. Dua after Durood-e-Ibraaheem

اَللّٰهُمَّ اغْفِرْ لِي مَا قَدَّمْتُ وَمَا أَخَّرْتُ وَمَا أَسْرَرْتُ وَمَا أَعْلَنْتُ وَمَا أَسْرَفْتُ وَمَا أَنْتَ أَعْلَمُ بِهِ مِنِّيْ أَنْتَ الْمُقَدِّمُ وَأَنْتَ الْمُؤَخِّرُ لَا إِلٰهَ إِلَّا أَنْتَ

O Allah! Forgive all those sins I may commit in the future and all those sins I have committed in the past, all those sins which I have done secretly and openly, all those sins I have done intentionally and all those sins which you alone know about me, you are well aware of the future and past, there is none worthy of worship besides You.

37. Azaan

اَللهُ اَكْبَرْ اَللهُ اَكْبَرْ   اَللهُ اَكْبَرْ اَللهُ اَكْبَرْ

Allah Ta'ala is the greatest.

اَشْهَدُ اَنْ لَّا اِلٰهَ اِلَّا الله   اَشْهَدُ اَنْ لَّا اِلٰهَ اِلَّا الله

I bear witness that there is no God besides Allah Ta'ala.

اَشْهَدُ اَنَّ مُحَمَّدًا رَّسُوْلُ الله   اَشْهَدُ اَنَّ مُحَمَّدًا رَّسُوْلُ الله

I bear witness that Muhammad ﷺ is the messenger of Allah Ta'ala.

حَيَّ عَلَى الصَّلٰوةْ   حَيَّ عَلَى الصَّلٰوةْ

Come to Salaah (Turn the face to the right when saying these words)

حَيَّ عَلَى الْفَلَاحْ   حَيَّ عَلَى الْفَلَاحْ

Come to success (Turn the face to the left when saying these words)

اَللهُ اَكْبَرْ   اَللهُ اَكْبَرْ

Allah Ta'ala is the greatest.

لَا اِلٰهَ اِلَّا الله

There is no God besides Allah Ta'ala.   *(Abu Dawood, Vol. 1, Pg. 79)*

38. Iqaamah

اَللّٰهُ اَكْبَرُ اللّٰهُ اَكْبَرُ

Allah Ta'ala is the greatest.

اَشْهَدُ اَنْ لَّا اِلٰهَ اِلَّا اللّٰهُ

I bear witness that there is no God besides Allah Ta'ala.

اَشْهَدُ اَنَّ مُحَمَّدًا رَّسُوْلُ اللّٰهِ

I bear witness that Muhammad ﷺ is the messenger of Allah Ta'ala.

حَىَّ عَلَى الصَّلٰوةِ

Come to Salaah (Turn the face to the right when saying these words)

حَىَّ عَلَى الْفَلَاحِ

Come to success (Turn the face to the left when saying these words)

قَدْ قَامَتِ الصَّلٰوةُ   قَدْ قَامَتِ الصَّلٰوةُ

Salaah is indeed about to begin

اَللّٰهُ اَكْبَرُ   اَللّٰهُ اَكْبَرُ

Allah Ta'ala is the greatest.

لَا اِلٰهَ اِلَّا اللّٰهُ

There is no God besides Allah Ta'ala.

Only in the Fajar Azaan, After saying:

$$\text{حَىَّ عَلَى الْفَلَاحُ}$$

The Muazzin will say

$$\text{اَلصَّلٰوةُ خَيْرٌ مِنَ النَّوْمِ اَلصَّلٰوةُ خَيْرٌ مِنَ النَّوْمِ}$$

Salaah is better than sleep

Aadaab (etiquettes) of Azaan

1. The Muazzin (person calling out the Azaan) should be in the state of wudhu when giving the Azaan.
2. He should face the Qiblah.
3. It is mustahab to put the forefingers in the ears when giving the Azaan.
4. The Azaan should be called out in a loud voice.
5. The Muazzin should pause between the words of the Azaan.
6. The Azaan should be called out from outside the boundaries of the masjid.
7. Azaan should be given from a high place, so that the voice can be heard at a distance.
8. When saying حَىَّ عَلَى الصَّلٰوةِ the face should be turned to the right.
9. When saying حَىَّ عَلَى الْفَلَاحِ the face should be turned to the left.

Note: Only the face should be turned. Not the chest or the feet.

39. Dua after Azaan

اَللّٰهُمَّ رَبَّ هٰذِهِ الدَّعْوَةِ التَّآمَّةِ وَالصَّلٰوةِ الْقَآئِمَةِ اٰتِ مُحَمَّدَ الْوَسِيْلَةَ وَالْفَضِيْلَةَ وَابْعَثْهُ مَقَامًا مَّحْمُوْدَ الَّذِىْ وَعَدْتَّهُ إِنَّكَ لَا تُخْلِفُ الْمِيْعَادَ

O Allah Ta'ala! The Rabb of this perfect call and everlasting salaah, grant our master Muhammad ﷺ the Waseelah and the virtue, and raise him to that praised position which You have promised him. Verily You do not go against Your promise. (Waseelah: a special place in Jannah)

(Sunnan-e-Baihaqi, Vol. 1, Pg. 410 / Abu Dawood, Vol. 1, Pg. 85)

Virtue:

Nabi ﷺ is reported to have said, "My intercession is necessary on the day of Qiyaamah for that person who recites durood shareef and then recites this dua after hearing the azaan."

Grade Three

GRADE 3

40. Before wudhu

بِسْمِ اللهِ وَالْحَمْدُ لِلّٰهِ

(I commence Wudhu), in the name of Allah Ta'ala and all praise be to Allah Ta'ala (for keeping me faithful in Islam).

(Majmauz-Zawaaid)

Virtue

Rasulullah ﷺ has said that a person who recites this dua before making wudhu, the angels continue writing down rewards for him as long as he/she remain in the state of wudhu.

41. Whilst making wudhu

اَللّٰهُمَّ اغْفِرْ لِيْ ذَنْبِيْ وَوَسِّعْ لِيْ فِيْ دَارِيْ وَبَارِكْ لِيْ فِيْ رِزْقِيْ

O Allah Ta'ala, forgive my sins and grant me abundance in my home and blessings in my livelihood.

(Amalul Yawmi wal Layla, Nasai, Pg172)

42. After wudhu

اَشْهَدُ اَنْ لَّا اِلٰهَ اِلَّا اللهُ وَحْدَهُ لَا شَرِيْكَ لَهُ وَاَشْهَدُ اَنَّ مُحَمَّدًا عَبْدُهُ وَرَسُوْلُهُ اَللّٰهُمَّ اجْعَلْنِيْ مِنَ التَّوَّابِيْنَ وَاجْعَلْنِيْ مِنَ الْمُتَطَهِّرِيْنَ

I bear witness that there is no God besides Allah Ta'ala. He is One. He has no partner. I bear witness that Hadhrat Muhammad ﷺ is His servant and messenger.
O Allah Ta'ala, make me of the repenters and make me of the purified ones.

(Tirmizi, Vol. 1, Pg. 9)

Virtue

The eight doors of Jannah will be opened for the one who recites this dua and he/she will have the choice to enter from whichever door he/she wishes.

43. When entering the Masjid

اَللّٰهُمَّ افْتَحْ لِیْ اَبْوَابَ رَحْمَتِكَ

O Allah Ta'ala, open for me the doors of Your mercy.

(Nasai, Vol. 1, Pg. 119)

44. When leaving the Masjid

اَللّٰهُمَّ اِنِّیْ اَسْئَلُكَ مِنْ فَضْلِكَ

O Allah Ta'ala, verily I seek from You, Your bounty.

(Nasai, Vol. 1, Pg. 119)

Aadaab of the Masjid

1. Make wudhu at home before going to the Masjid.
2. Enter the Masjid with the right foot.
3. Do not talk in the Masjid.
4. Do not walk in front of those performing salaah.
5. Do not dirty or leave dirt lying around in the Masjid.
6. Leave the Masjid with the left foot.
7. Make sure your cell phone is switched off before entering the Masjid.

45. After drinking water

$$\text{اَلْحَمْدُ لِلهِ الَّذِىْ سَقَانَا عَذْبًا فُرَاتًاۢ بِرَحْمَتِهٖ وَلَمْ يَجْعَلْهُ مِلْحًا اُجَاجًاۢ بِذُنُوْبِنَا}$$

All praise is due to Allah Ta'ala who gave us fresh sweet water to drink out of His Mercy and did not make it bitter due to our wrongdoings.

(Tabraani {Kitaabud-Dua}, Vol. 2, Pg. 1218)

Sunnats of Drinking

1. A Muslim should drink with the right hand.
2. Sit and drink.
3. Recite *"Bismillah"* before drinking.
4. After drinking say *"Alhamdulillah"*.
5. Drink in 3 breaths removing the utensil from the mouth after each sip.
6. Do not drink directly from the jug or bottle. One should pour the contents into a glass first and then drink.

46. After drinking milk

اَللّٰهُمَّ بَارِكْ لَنَا فِيْهِ وَزِدْنَا مِنْهُ

O Allah Ta'ala, grant us blessings and abundance in this (milk).

(Mishkaat Pg.371)

47. When wearing clothes

اَلْحَمْدُ لِلّٰهِ الَّذِىْ كَسَانِىْ هٰذَا وَرَزَقَنِيْهِ مِنْ غَيْرِ حَوْلٍ مِنِّىْ وَلَاقُوَّةٍ

All praise is due to Allah Ta'ala who has clothed me with these garments and given them to me without any effort and help from my side.

(Tabraani {Kitaabud-Dua}, Vol. 2, Pg. 979)

48. When looking into the mirror

اَللّٰهُمَّ اَنْتَ حَسَّنْتَ خَلْقِىْ فَحَسِّنْ خُلُقِىْ

O Allah Ta'ala, You have beautified my body, so do beautify my character.

(Al-Hisnul Haseen Pg. 206)

49. When entering the home

$$\text{اَللّٰهُمَّ اِنِّیْ اَسْئَلُكَ خَیْرَ الْمَوْلَجِ وَخَیْرَ الْمَخْرَجِ بِسْمِ اللهِ وَلَجْنَا وَبِسْمِ اللهِ خَرَجْنَا وَعَلَى اللهِ رَبَّنَا تَوَكَّلْنَا}$$

O Allah Ta'ala, I ask of You the blessings of entering the home and the blessing of leaving. In the name of Allah Ta'ala, we enter and In the name of Allah Ta'ala, we leave the home and upon Allah Ta'ala, our Sustainer, do we rely and depend.

(Abu Dawood, Vol. 2, Pg. 348)

Aadaab of entering the home

1. Recite the dua before entering the home.
2. Greet those that are in the house with *"Assalaamu alaykum."*
3. Announce ones arrival by coughing, greeting etc. even though it may be your own house.

50. When leaving the home

بِسْمِ اللهِ تَوَكَّلْتُ عَلَى اللهِ لَاحَوْلَ وَلَاقُوَّةَ اِلَّا بِاللهِ

(I leave) with the name of Allah Ta'ala; I rely on Allah Ta'ala; there is no power to do any good, nor any power to abstain from evil except with the help of Allah Ta'ala.

(Abu Dawood, Vol. 2, Pg. 347)

Virtue

Rasulullah ﷺ said that whosoever recites the above dua when leaving his home, then it is said to him (by the angels) "You shall be guided, your needs shall be taken care of, you will be protected and may shaytaan go far away from you."

(Tirmizi)

51. When bidding someone farewell

اَسْتَوْدِعُ اللّٰهَ دِيْنَكَ وَاَمَانَتَكَ وَخَوَاتِيْمَ عَمَلِكَ

I entrust your Deen, your belongings and the final outcome of your deeds to Allah Ta'ala.

(Abu Dawood, Vol. 1, Pg. 357)

52. When it rains

اَللّٰهُمَّ صَيِّبًا نَّافِعًا

O Allah Ta'ala, do send upon us beneficial rain.

(Bukhaari, Vol. 1, Pg. 140)

GRADE 3

53. On hearing good news

اَلْحَمْدُ لِلّٰهِ مَاشَاءَ اللهُ

All praise be to Allah Ta'ala, just as Allah Ta'ala willed.

54. When a loss occurs

اِنَّا لِلّٰهِ وَ اِنَّآ اِلَيْهِ رَاجِعُوْنَ

Surely we belong to Allah Ta'ala and to Him is our return.

(Muslim, Vol. 1 Pg. 300)

Virtue

Rasulullah H said, "When a person reads "Inna lillahi wa innaa ilayhi rajioon" at the time of a calamity, Allah Ta'ala gives him a better recompense over his loss in this world and stores his reward for him in the hereafter."

55. When in bodily pain

Place your hand on the affected area and say:

$$\text{بِسْمِ اللهِ}$$

(Three Times)

$$\text{اَعُوْذُ بِاللهِ وَقُدْرَتِهٖ مِنْ شَرِّ مَا اَجِدُ وَاُحَاذِرُ}$$

(Seven times)

I seek protection in Allah Ta'ala and His might against the evil of what I feel and fear.

(Muslim, Vol. 2, Pg. 224)

56. When in difficulty

$$\text{حَسْبُنَا اللهُ وَنِعْمَ الْوَكِيْلُ وَ عَلَى اللهِ تَوَكَّلْنَا}$$

Allah Ta'ala is sufficient for us and He is the Best Helper. And upon Allah Ta'ala do we rely.

(Tirmizi, Vol. 2, Pg. 65)

57. Dua for death on Imaan

رَبَّنَا لَا تُزِغْ قُلُوْبَنَا بَعْدَ اِذْ هَدَيْتَنَا وَهَبْ لَنَا مِنْ لَّدُنْكَ رَحْمَةً اِنَّكَ اَنْتَ الْوَهَّابُ

O Our Rabb! Do not let our hearts go astray after You have granted us guidance, and grant us mercy from Your side. Verily You are The Great Giver of favours.

(AL-Qur-aan S. 03, V. 08)

58. When getting into a vehicle

بِسْمِ اللهِ اَلْحَمْدُ لِلّٰهِ سُبْحَانَ الَّذِىْ سَخَّرَلَنَا هٰذَا وَمَا كُنَّا لَهُ مُقْرِنِيْنَ وَاِنَّاۤ اِلٰى رَبِّنَا لَمُنْقَلِبُوْنَ

All praise be to Allah Ta'ala, Glory be to Allah Ta'ala who has put this (vehicle) under our control though we were unable to control it. Surely, to our Sustainer are we to return.

(Tirmizi, Vol. 2, Pg. 182)

59. When the vehicle moves

بِسْمِ اللهِ مَجْرِهَا وَمُرْسَهَا اِنَّ رَبِّيْ لَغَفُوْرٌ رَّحِيْمٌ

Note: The Raa in مَجْ is pronounced as "Re" as in the word "Red"

In the name of Allah Ta'ala is its moving and its stopping. Most certainly, my Rabb is most Forgiving, Most Merciful.

(Al-Qur-aan S.11 V.41)

60. When returning from a journey

اٰئِبُوْنَ تَائِبُوْنَ عَابِدُوْنَ لِرَبِّنَا حَامِدُوْنَ

We are returning, we are repenting, we worship (Allah Ta'ala), and praise our sustainer.

(Muslim Vol. 1, Pg. 434)

61. When entering a town or city

Recite three times

اَللّٰهُمَّ بَارِكْ لَنَا فِيهَا

Thereafter recite

اَللّٰهُمَّ ارْزُقْنَا جَنَاهَا وَ حَبِّبْنَا اِلٰى اَهْلِهَا وَحَبِّبْ صَالِحِىْ اَهْلِهَا اِلَيْنَا

O Allah Ta'ala! Grant us barakat (blessing) in this place. O Allah Ta'ala! Give us of its produce and make us liked by its people and create the love of its pious people in us.

(Al Mu'jamul Awsat Vol. 5, Pg. 379)

62. Dua-e-Qunoot

اَللّٰهُمَّ اهْدِنِيْ فِيْمَنْ هَدَيْتَ اٰمِيْن وَعَافِنِيْ فِيْمَنْ عَافَيْتَ اٰمِيْن وَتَوَلَّنِيْ فِيْمَنْ تَوَلَّيْتَ اٰمِيْن وَبَارِكْ لِيْ فِيْمَا أَعْطَيْتَ اٰمِيْن وَقِنِيْ شَرَّ مَا قَضَيْتَ اٰمِيْن فَإِنَّكَ تَقْضِيْ وَلَا يُقْضٰى عَلَيْكَ وَإِنَّهُ لَا يَذِلُّ مَنْ وَّالَيْتَ وَلَا يَعِزُّ مَنْ عَادَيْتَ تَبَارَكْتَ رَبَّنَا وَتَعَالَيْتَ فَلَكَ الْحَمْدُ عَلٰى مَا قَضَيْتَ أَسْتَغْفِرُكَ وَأَتُوْبُ إِلَيْكَ وَصَلَّى اللّٰهُ عَلٰى سَيِّدِنَا مُحَمَّدٍ وَّعَلٰى اٰلِهِ وَصَحْبِهِ وَسَلَّمَ.

GRADE 4

O Allah! Guide me amongst those whom You have guided aright, And preserve me amongst those whom You have preserved. Take me for a friend amongst those whom You have taken for friends. Bless me in that which You have bestowed upon me. Guard me from the evil of that which You have ordained. For, behold, it is You who ordains and none can ordain against You. Never is he disgraced whom You take for a friend, and he is never honoured from whom You have turned. Our sustainer, blessed and exalted are You! Praise is due to you on that which You have ordained. I beg forgiveness of You and repent before You, and may the blessings of Allah be showered upon our Noble Muhammad (sallallahu alayhi wasallam), his descendants and companions, and may peace be upon them all.

Note: Qunoot will be read everyday in the Qaumah of the 2nd Rakaat of Fajr Salaah and, from the 16th night of Ramadhan till the end of Ramadhan Qunoot will be read in the Qaumah of the third Rakaat of the Witr Salaah.

63. Dua after Witr Salaah

سُبْحَانَ الْمَلِكِ الْقُدُّوْسِ

Glory be to Allah Ta'ala the Most Holy King.

(Nasai, Vol. 1, Pg. 253)

Note:

Recite the above dua three times and on the third time raise your voice slightly and pull the daal and the waw in Quddoos.

64. On seeing the new moon

اَللّٰهُمَّ اَهِلَّهُ عَلَيْنَا بِالْيُمْنِ وَالْاِيْمَانِ وَالسَّلَامَةِ وَالْاِسْلَامِ وَالتَّوْفِيْقِ لِمَا تُحِبُّ وَتَرْضٰى رَبِّيْ وَرَبُّكَ الله

O Allah Ta'ala let this new moon appear to us with prosperity, faith, safety and Islam and with the hope of success to do deeds which You would like and approve of. My Lord and Your Lord (O Moon!) is Allah Ta'ala.

(Tirmizi, Vol. 2, Pg. 183)

65. Dua for fasting

اَللّٰهُمَّ اَصُوْمُ غَدًا لَكَ فَاغْفِرْلِىْ مَا قَدَّمْتُ وَمَا اَخَّرْتُ

O Allah Ta'ala! I shall fast tomorrow for Your sake, so forgive my past and future sins.

Alternative recite this dua

بِصَوْمِ غَدٍ نَّوَيْتُ

I intend fasting tomorrow.

Hadith

Rasulullah ﷺ has said: "Eat sehri because in it lies great blessings."

GRADE 4

66. When breaking the fast

اَللّٰهُمَّ لَكَ صُمْتُ وَبِكَ اٰمَنْتُ وَعَلٰى رِزْقِكَ اَفْطَرْتُ

O Allah Ta'ala, I fasted for You. In You do I believe, and with Your provision (food) do I break my fast.

(Kitaabud-Dua Tabraani, Vol. 2, Pg. 1229)

Hadith

Rasulullah ﷺ said: "Fasting is a protective shield for man."

Do's	Don'ts
· Do Fast in the month of Ramadhaan.	· Don't commit sinful acts.
· Do offer Tahajjud Salaah before sehri ends.	· Don't break your fast before time.
· Do increase the performance of Nafl Salaah.	· Don't miss Taraaweeh Salaah.
· Do recite the Qur'aan as much as one can.	· Don't watch T.V., videos, DVDs, etc.
· Do increase in making Zikr.	· Don't listen to music.
· Do engage in Dua excessively.	· Don't swear, speak lies or backbite others.
· Do increase in giving Sadaqah (charity).	· Don't engage in unnecessary actions.
· Do sit for I'tikaaf in the last ten days of Ramadhaan.	· Don't miss out any of your salaah.
· Do make a firm intention to change your life in Ramadhaan FOREVER.	

67. When eating elsewhere (1)

$$\text{اَللّٰهُمَّ بَارِكْ لَهُمْ فِيمَا رَزَقْتَهُمْ وَاغْفِرْ لَهُمْ وَارْحَمْهُمْ}$$

O Allah Ta'ala, bless them in what You have provided them with and forgive them and have mercy upon them.

(Muslim, Vol. 2, Pg. 180)

Hadith:

Rasulullah ﷺ has said: "When Allah Ta'ala intends good for a person, He gives him a gift in the form of a guest. The guest comes with his own rizq and when he leaves, the whole family (of the host) is forgiven."

68. When eating elsewhere (2)

اَكَلَ طَعَامَكُمُ الْاَبْرَارُ وَصَلَّتْ عَلَيْكُمُ الْمَلَائِكَةُ وَاَفْطَرَ عِنْدَكُمُ الصَّائِمُوْنَ

May the righteous partake of your food. May the angels of mercy and may the fasting ones break their fast at your place.

(Musnad-e-Ahmad 12429 Vol. 3 Pg 138)

69. When eating the first fruit of the season

اَللّٰهُمَّ بَارِكْ لَنَا فِىْ ثَمَرِنَا وَبَارِكْ لَنَا فِىْ مَدِيْنَتِنَا وَبَارِكْ لَنَا فِىْ صَاعِنَا وَبَارِكْ لَنَا فِىْ مُدِّنَا

O Allah Ta'ala, grant us abundance in our fruit and bless us in our town and bless us in our weight and our measure.

(Muslim, Vol. 1, Pg. 442)

Note:

When the first fruit of the season is brought, it should first be given to the youngest child present to eat.

70. Dua when afflicted with some calamity

$$\text{اَللّٰهُمَّ اْجُرْنِىْ فِىْ مُصِيْبَتِىْ وَ اَخْلِفْ لِىْ خَيْرًا مِّنْهَا}$$

O Allah Ta'ala: Reward me in this difficulty of mine and grant me something even better in return.

(Muslim Vol. 1, Pg. 300)

Virtue

Nabi ﷺ said: "Whoever reads this dua whilst in difficulty, Allah Ta'ala will replace him with something better."

(Mishkaat Pg. 140)

71. When in financial difficulty

اَللّٰهُمَّ اكْفِنِيْ بِحَلَالِكَ عَنْ حَرَامِكَ وَاَغْنِنِيْ بِفَضْلِكَ عَمَّنْ سِوَاكَ

O Allah Ta'ala, provide me with sufficient halaal livelihood, save me from that which You declared as Haraam and through Your grace protect me from asking anyone besides Yourself.

(Tirmizi Vol. 2, Pg. 195)

72. When seeing someone in distress (say softly)

اَلْحَمْدُ لِلّٰهِ الَّذِیْ عَافَانِیْ مِمَّا ابْتَلَاكَ بِهٖ وَفَضَّلَنِیْ عَلٰی كَثِیْرٍ مِّمَّنْ خَلَقَ تَفْضِیْلًا

All praise is due to Allah Ta'ala who saved me from what He has tested you with and He has blessed me with special favours compared to many of His creation.

(Tirmizi, Vol. 2, Pg. 181)

73. Dua for fever

بِسْمِ اللهِ الْكَبِيرِ اَعُوذُ بِاللهِ الْعَظِيْمِ مِنْ شَرِّ كُلِّ عِرْقٍ نَّعَّارٍ وَّ مِنْ شَرِّ حَرِّ النَّارِ

With the name of Allah Ta'ala, the Great, I seek protection in Allah Ta'ala, The Magnificent, from the evil of every spurting vein and from the severe heat of the fire.

(Mujamul Kabir Tabraani, Vol. 11, Pg. 225)

74. When visiting the sick

لَابَأْسَ طَهُوْرٌ اِنْ شَاءَ اللهُ

اَللّٰهُمَّ اشْفِهِ اَللّٰهُمَّ عَافِهِ

Do not despair, it is a cleansing (from sins) if Allah Ta'ala wills; O Allah Ta'ala, grant him cure and ease.

(Bukhaari Vol. 2 Pg. 845)

Virtue:

Rasulullah ﷺ has said: "One who visits a sick person in the morning, 70 000 angels make *du'a-e-rahmah* (*du'a* of mercy) for him till the evening and that person who visits a sick person in the evening; 70,000 angels make *du'a-e-rahmah* for him until the morning."

Rasulullah ﷺ has said that whosoever visits a sick person, an angel calls out from the sky: "You have done well. Your walking is also good and you have built yourself a palace in *Jannah*."

75. At the time of death

$$\text{لَا اِلٰهَ اِلَّا اللهُ مُحَمَّدٌ رَّسُوْلُ اللهِ}$$

$$\text{اَللّٰهُمَّ اَعِنِّىْ عَلٰى غَمَرَاتِ الْمَوْتِ}$$

$$\text{وَسَكَرَاتِ الْمَوْتِ}$$

There is no God besides Allah Ta'ala. Muhammad ﷺ is His messenger. O Allah Ta'ala, help me to overcome the agonies and difficulties of death.

(Tirmizi Vol. 1, Pg. 117)

Note:

When the time draws near for a person to pass away, those around him should encourage him to recite the kalimah by reciting it in a soft voice.

76. After 2nd Takbeer in Janazah Salaah

اَللّٰهُمَّ صَلِّ عَلٰى سَيِّدِنَا مُحَمَّدٍ وَّعَلٰى اٰلِ مُحَمَّدٍ كَمَا صَلَّيْتَ عَلٰى اِبْرَاهِيْمَ وَعَلٰى اٰلِ اِبْرَاهِيْمَ وَبَارِكْ عَلٰى مُحَمَّدٍ وَّعَلٰى اٰلِ مُحَمَّدٍ كَمَا بَارَكْتَ عَلٰى اِبْرَاهِيْمَ وَعَلٰى اٰلِ اِبْرَاهِيْمَ فِى الْعَالَمِيْنَ اِنَّكَ حَمِيْدٌ مَّجِيْدٌ

O Allah Ta'ala! Shower Your mercy on Muhammad ﷺ and his family (followers) as You showered Your mercy on Ibraaheem عَلَيْهِ السَّلَام and his family (followers). And bless Muhammad ﷺ and his family (followers) as You have blessed Ibraaheem عَلَيْهِ السَّلَام and his family (followers) in the worlds. Surely You are Praiseworthy and Most High.

Note:
Recite Surah Faatihah after the first Takbeer in Janazah Salaah

77. After 3rd Takbeer in Janazah Salaah

اَللّٰهُمَّ اغْفِرْ لِحَيِّنَا وَمَيِّتِنَا وَشَاهِدِنَا وَغَائِبِنَا وَصَغِيرِنَا وَكَبِيرِنَا وَذَكَرِنَا وَأُنْثَانَا اَللّٰهُمَّ مَنْ اَحْيَيْتَهُ مِنَّا فَاَحْيِهٖ عَلَى الْاِسْلَامِ وَمَنْ تَوَفَّيْتَهُ مِنَّا فَتَوَفَّهُ عَلَى الْاِيْمَانِ

O Allah Ta'ala, forgive amongst us those who are alive and those who are dead, those who are present and those who are absent, those who are young and those who are old, those who are males and those who are females. O Allah Ta'ala, whom You keep alive amongst us, keep him alive upon Islam and whom You caused to die, let him die upon Imaan.

(Tirmizi, Vol. 1, Pg. 121)

78. After 4th Takbeer in Janazah Salaah

اَللّٰهُمَّ لَا تَحْرِمْنَا اَجْرَهُ وَلَا تَفْتِنَّا بَعْدَهُ وَاغْفِرْ لَنَا وَلَهُ

O Allah! Do not deprive us of his reward and do not make us be put into trails after him and forgive us and him.

79. When entering the graveyard

اَلسَّلَامُ عَلَيْكُمْ اَهْلَ الدِّيَارِ مِنَ الْمُؤْمِنِيْنَ وَالْمُسْلِمِيْنَ وَاِنَّا اِنْ شَآءَ اللهُ بِكُمْ لَاحِقُوْنَ نَسْأَلُ اللهَ لَنَا وَلَكُمُ الْعَافِيَةَ

Peace be upon you O Mu'mineen and Muslimeen who dwell herein. Insha Allah Ta'ala we shall join you. We ask Allah Ta'ala ease for us and for you.

(Ibnu Majah, Pg.111)

80. Dua to be recited in the Graveyard

اَللّٰهُمَّ اغْفِرْلَهُ وَارْحَمْهُ وَعَافِهِ وَاعْفُ عَنْهُ وَأَكْرِمْ نُزُلَهُ وَوَسِّعْ مَدْخَلَهُ وَاغْسِلْهُ بِالْمَاءِ وَالثَّلْجِ وَالْبَرَدِ وَنَقِّهِ مِنَ الْخَطَايَا كَمَا نَقَّيْتَ الثَّوْبَ الْأَبْيَضَ مِنَ الدَّنَسِ وَأَبْدِلْهُ دَارًا خَيْرًا مِّنْ دَارِهِ وَأَهْلًا خَيْرًا مِّنْ أَهْلِهِ وَزَوْجًا خَيْرًا مِّنْ زَوْجِهِ وَأَدْخِلْهُ الْجَنَّةَ وَأَعِذْهُ مِنْ عَذَابِ الْقَبْرِ وَعَذَابِ النَّارِ

O Allah! Forgive him. Have mercy upon him. Give him peace and absolve him. Receive him honourably, and make his grave spacious. Wash him with water, snow and hail. Cleanse him from faults as You cleanse a white garment from impurity. Replace him with an abode better than his abode, with a household better than his household. Admit him to Jannah and protect him from the torment of the grave and punishment of the Fire. *(Muslim)*

81. When laying the dead into the grave

بِسْمِ اللهِ وَعَلٰى مِلَّةِ رَسُوْلِ اللهِ

In the name of Allah Ta'ala and in the manner of Rasulullah ﷺ (do we lay this body to rest).

(Ibnu Majah, Pg.111)

Note

Rasulullah ﷺ has said: "Visit the graves, for surely visiting the graves, decreases the love for the world and reminds you of the hereafter."

N.B. Only males are allowed to visit the graveyard.

82. When filling the qabar with soil

When throwing the first handful (of soil), say:

مِنْهَا خَلَقْنَاكُمْ

From sand did We create you.

When throwing the second handful, say:

وَفِيْهَا نُعِيْدُكُمْ

And to sand shall We return you.

When throwing the third handful, say:

وَمِنْهَا نُخْرِجُكُمْ تَارَةً اُخْرٰى

And from the sand shall We raise you once again.

(Mustadrak Haakim, Vol. 2, Pg. 379)

GRADE 6

83. At the time of sunset

$$\text{اَللّٰهُمَّ هٰذَا اِقْبَالُ لَيْلِكَ وَاِدْبَارُ نَهَارِكَ وَاَصْوَاتُ دُعَاتِكَ فَاغْفِرْلِيْ}$$

O Allah Ta'ala, this is the approaching of Your night and the disappearing of Your day and the voices of those who call (referring to Adhaan) to You. So do forgive me.

(Miskhaat, Pg. 660)

84. When seeing the moon

$$\text{اَعُوْذُ بِاللّٰهِ مِنْ شَرِّ هٰذَا الْغَاسِقِ}$$

I seek the protection of Allah Ta'ala from the evil of this dark moon.

(Tirmizi, Vol. 2, Pg. 172)

85. At the time of drought

اَللّٰهُمَّ اسْقِنَا اَللّٰهُمَّ اَغِثْنَا

O Allah Ta'ala, quench our thirst, O Allah Ta'ala, send us rain.

(Tirmizi, Vol. 2, Pg. 66)

86. When there is excessive rain

اَللّٰهُمَّ حَوَالَيْنَا وَلَا عَلَيْنَا اَللّٰهُمَّ عَلَى الْاٰكَامِ وَالْاٰجَامِ وَالظِّرَابِ وَالْاَوْدِيَةِ وَمَنَابِتِ الشَّجَرِ

O Allah Ta'ala, send rain in the outskirts, not upon us. O Allah Ta'ala, make it rain upon the hills, in the woods, on the mountains, in the valleys and gardens and orchards.

(Bukhaari, Vol. 1, Pg. 138)

87. When wearing new clothes

$$\text{اَلْحَمْدُ لِلّٰهِ الَّذِىْ كَسَانِىْ مَا أُوَارِىْ بِهٖ عَوْرَتِىْ وَاَتَجَمَّلُ بِهٖ فِىْ حَيَاتِىْ}$$

Praise be to Allah Ta'ala, who clothed me with that which I cover my shame and adorn myself during my life.

(Tirmizi, Vol. 2, Pg. 195)

Virtue

It is mentioned in the Hadith that if a person recites this dua after wearing new clothes and he gives his old clothes in sadaqah (charity), then he will be in the guardianship and protection of Allah Ta'ala.

(Tirmizi)

88. Dua when leaving a gathering

سُبْحَانَ اللّٰهِ وَبِحَمْدِهٖ سُبْحَانَكَ اللّٰهُمَّ وَبِحَمْدِكَ اَشْهَدُ اَنْ لَّا اِلٰهَ اِلَّا اَنْتَ اَسْتَغْفِرُكَ وَاَتُوْبُ اِلَيْكَ

Glory be to Allah Ta'ala with His praises. Glory be to You, O Allah Ta'ala, with Your praises I bear witness that there is no God besides You. I beg Your forgiveness and repent to You.

(Mustadrak Haakim, Vol. 1, Pg. 537)

Virtue

Whosoever recites the following dua after sitting in a gathering will be forgiven for whatever wrongs were done in that gathering.

(Abu Dawood Pg. 681)

89. When entering a shopping centre

لَا اِلٰهَ اِلَّا اللهُ وَحْدَهُ لَا شَرِيكَ لَهُ لَهُ الْمُلْكُ وَلَهُ الْحَمْدُ يُحْيِي وَيُمِيتُ وَهُوَ حَيٌّ لَا يَمُوتُ بِيَدِهِ الْخَيْرُ وَهُوَ عَلَىٰ كُلِّ شَيْءٍ قَدِيرٌ

There is no God besides Allah Ta'ala. He is One. He has no partner. For him is the kingdom and for Him is all praise. He gives life and causes death. He is Ever living and never dies. In His hand is all good. And He has power over everything.

(Tirmizi, Vol. 2, Pg. 180)

Virtue

Whosoever recites the above dua will receive one million rewards, one million of his sins will be wiped out and his ranks will be raised a million times. Furthermore a palace will be built for him in Jannah.

(Tirmizi)

Rasulullah ﷺ said: "The best of places unto Allah Ta'ala are the masaajid and the worst of places in the sight of Allah are the shopping centers."

(Mishkaat)

90. The 99 beautiful names of Allah Ta'ala

هُوَ اللهُ الَّذِى لَآ اِلٰهَ اِلَّا هُوَ

Allah سُبْحَانَهُ وَتَعَالَى is He besides whom there is no God but Him

الْمُؤْمِنُ	السَّلَامُ	الْقُدُّوسُ	الْمَلِكُ	الرَّحِيمُ	الرَّحْمٰنُ	
الْبَارِئُ	الْخَالِقُ	الْمُتَكَبِّرُ	الْجَبَّارُ	الْعَزِيزُ	الْمُهَيْمِنُ	
الْفَتَّاحُ	الرَّزَّاقُ	الْوَهَّابُ	الْقَهَّارُ	الْغَفَّارُ	الْمُصَوِّرُ	
الْمُعِزُّ	الرَّافِعُ	الْخَافِضُ	الْبَاسِطُ	الْقَابِضُ	الْعَلِيمُ	
اللَّطِيفُ	الْعَدْلُ	الْحَكَمُ	الْبَصِيرُ	السَّمِيعُ	الْمُذِلُّ	
الْعَلِيُّ	الشَّكُورُ	الْغَفُورُ	الْعَظِيمُ	الْحَلِيمُ	الْخَبِيرُ	
الْكَرِيمُ	الْجَلِيلُ	الْحَسِيبُ	الْمُقِيتُ	الْحَفِيظُ	الْكَبِيرُ	
الْمَجِيدُ	الْوَدُودُ	الْحَكِيمُ	الْوَاسِعُ	الْمُجِيبُ	الرَّقِيبُ	

GRADE 6

الْمَتِيْنُ	الْقَوِيُّ	الْوَكِيْلُ	الْحَقُّ	الشَّهِيْدُ	الْبَاعِثُ
الْمُحْيِي	الْمُعِيْدُ	الْمُبْدِئُ	الْمُحْصِى	الْحَمِيْدُ	الْوَلِيُّ
الْوَاحِدُ	الْمَاجِدُ	الْوَاجِدُ	الْقَيُّوْمُ	الْحَيُّ	الْمُمِيْتُ
الْمُؤَخِّرُ	الْمُقَدِّمُ	الْمُقْتَدِرُ	الْقَادِرُ	الصَّمَدُ	الْأَحَدُ
الْمُتَعَالِي	الْوَالِي	الْبَاطِنُ	الظَّاهِرُ	الْأَخِرُ	الْأَوَّلُ
	الرَّؤُوْفُ	الْعَفُوُّ	الْمُنْتَقِمُ	التَّوَّابُ	الْبَرُّ
الْجَامِعُ	الْمُقْسِطُ	ذُوالْجَلَالِ وَالْاِكْرَامِ		مَالِكُ الْمُلْكِ	
النُّوْرُ	النَّافِعُ	الضَّآرُّ	الْمَانِعُ	الْمُغْنِي	الْغَنِيُّ
الصَّبُوْرُ	الرَّشِيْدُ	الْوَارِثُ	الْبَاقِي	الْبَدِيْعُ	الْهَادِي

Virtue:

Rasulullah ﷺ said: "Verily Allah Ta'ala has 99 names. Whosoever memorises them will enter Jannah."

91. When laying the Qurbaani animal down for slaughtering

$$\text{اِنِّیْ وَجَّهْتُ وَجْهِیَ لِلَّذِیْ فَطَرَ السَّمٰوٰتِ وَالْاَرْضَ عَلٰی مِلَّةِ اِبْرَاهِیْمَ حَنِیْفًا وَّ مَآ اَنَاْ مِنَ الْمُشْرِكِیْنَ}$$

I have firmly turned myself towards that Being Who has created the heavens and the earth, while I am upon the Straight Deen of Hadhrat Ibraaheem عَلَيْهِ ٱلسَّلَام, and I am not among the Mushrikeen.

اِنَّ صَلَاتِيْ وَ نُسُكِيْ وَ مَحْيَايَ وَ مَمَاتِيْ لِلّٰهِ رَبِّ الْعَالَمِيْنَ لَا شَرِيْكَ لَهُ وَ بِذَالِكَ اُمِرْتُ وَ اَنَا مِنَ الْمُسْلِمِيْنَ

اَللّٰهُمَّ مِنْكَ وَلَكَ عَنْ.........

Verily, my Salaah, my sacrifice, my life and my death are for Allah Ta'ala, Rabb of the worlds. He has no partner, with this I have been commanded and I am the first of those who surrender. O Allah Ta'ala! This sacrifice is due to You granting us the ability to do so and it is for You.

Note:

After saying the word "عَنْ" mention the name of the person on whose behalf the sacrifice is being made.

92. When slaughtering the animal

$$\text{بِسْمِ اللهِ اَللهُ اَكْبَرُ}$$

In the name of Allah Ta'ala, Allah Ta'ala is the greatest.

(Mishkaat Pg.128)

93. Sayyidul Istighfaar

اَللّٰهُمَّ اَنْتَ رَبِّيْ لَا اِلٰهَ اِلَّا اَنْتَ خَلَقْتَنِيْ وَاَنَا عَبْدُكَ وَاَنَا عَلٰى عَهْدِكَ وَوَعْدِكَ مَا اسْتَطَعْتُ اَعُوْذُ بِكَ مِنْ شَرِّ مَا صَنَعْتُ اَبُوْءُ لَكَ بِنِعْمَتِكَ عَلَىَّ وَاَبُوْءُ بِذَنْۢبِيْ فَاغْفِرْلِيْ فَاِنَّهُ لَا يَغْفِرُ الذُّنُوْبَ اِلَّا اَنْتَ

O Allah Ta'ala, You are my Cherisher. There is no god except You. You have created me and I am your servant. As far as possible, I abide by my solemn promise and covenant (which I made to You). I seek Your protection against the consequences of my wrongdoings. I fully acknowledge the grace you have bestowed upon me and confess my faults. So please forgive me as none besides you can pardon sins.

(Bukhaari, Vol. 2, Pg. 933)

Virtue

The person who recites this dua sincerely in the course of the day and night and dies will be among the people of Jannah.

(Bukhaari)

Note

1. Every Muslim should at least make Istighfaar 100 times daily.
2. We all are sinners and must make Istighfaar.
3. Allah Ta'ala loves those who repent.
4. If we commit a sin we should immediately make Istighfaar and ask for forgiveness.

94. Dua for Istikhaarah

اَللّٰهُمَّ اِنِّىْ اَسْتَخِيْرُكَ بِعِلْمِكَ وَاَسْتَقْدِرُكَ بِقُدْرَتِكَ وَاَسْئَلُكَ مِنْ فَضْلِكَ الْعَظِيْمِ فَاِنَّكَ تَقْدِرُ وَلَا اَقْدِرُ وَتَعْلَمُ وَلَا اَعْلَمُ وَاَنْتَ عَلَّامُ الْغُيُوْبِ اَللّٰهُمَّ اِنْ كُنْتَ تَعْلَمُ اَنَّ هٰذَا الْاَمَرَ خَيْرٌ لِّىْ فِىْ دِيْنِىْ وَمَعَاشِىْ وَعَاقِبَةِ اَمْرِىْ فَاقْدُرْهُ لِىْ وَيَسِّرْهُ لِىْ ثُمَّ بَارِكْ لِىْ فِيْهِ وَاِنْ كُنْتَ تَعْلَمُ اَنَّ هٰذَا الْاَمَرَ شَرٌّ لِّىْ فِىْ دِيْنِىْ وَمَعَاشِىْ وَعَاقِبَةِ اَمْرِىْ فَاصْرِفْهُ عَنِّىْ وَاصْرِفْنِىْ عَنْهُ وَاقْدُرْ لِىَ الْخَيْرَ حَيْثُ كَانَ ثُمَّ اَرْضِنِىْ بِهٖ

GRADE 7

O Allah Ta'ala, I ask You for good through Your knowledge and I ask You for ability through Your power and I beg (Your favour) out of Your infinite bounty. Surely, You have power and I have none. You know everything and I know not. You are the great knower of all things. O Allah Ta'ala, if, in Your sublime knowledge, this matter is good for my faith (Deen), for my livelihood and for the consequences of my affairs, then decree it for me and make it easy for me and bless me therein. But if, in Your knowledge, this matter is bad for my faith (Deen), for my livelihood and for the consequences of my affairs, then turn it away from me and turn me away there from and ordain for me the good wherever it be and cause me to be pleased therewith.

(Bukhaari, Vol. 1, Pg. 155)

Note:

While reciting this dua, on reaching the highlighted words, one should think of and mention one's problem in any language. Thereafter, do whatever one feels suitable. It is not necessary that one will see a special dream.

(Istikhaarah should be made for all important matters.)

GRADE 7

Alternatively, one may recite the following dua 11 times.

$$\text{اَللّٰهُمَّ خِرْ لِي وَاخْتَرْ لِي}$$

O Allah please choose and select things for me that is in my best interest and favour me with the same.

95. The most comprehensive of all duas

Hadhrat Abu Umaamah ﷺ narrates that Nabi ﷺ made lots of duas which we were unable to memorise. We said: "O Nabi of Allah ﷺ, You have made many duas which we were unable to memories. Can you not teach us such a dua that would encompass all of it." Rasulullah ﷺ said: Recite...

اَللّٰهُمَّ اِنَّا نَسْئَلُكَ مِنْ خَيْرِ مَا سَئَلَكَ مِنْهُ نَبِيُّكَ مُحَمَّدٌ صَلَّى اللهُ عَلَيْهِ وَ سَلَّم وَنَعُوْذُ بِكَ مِنْ شَرِّ مَا اسْتَعَاذَ مِنْهُ نَبِيُّكَ مُحَمَّدٌ صَلَّى اللهُ عَلَيْهِ وَ سَلَّم وَ اَنْتَ الْمُسْتَعَانُ وَ عَلَيْكَ الْبَلَاغُ وَ لَا حَوْلَ ولَاقُوَّةَ اِلَّا بِاللهِ

O Allah, Verily we ask of You all the good that Hadhrat Muhammad ﷺ had asked of You and we seek protection in You from all the evil that Hadhrat Muhammad ﷺ had sought protection in You from. It is only You from whom we can seek assistance and it is only You who can fulfil our dua and there is no power to do good nor any power to prevent from evil except with Allah Ta'ala.

(Tirmizi Vol. 2, Pg. 192)

Etiquettes of Dua

1. Every Muslim must make dua and beg Allah Ta'ala for his needs.
2. Be in the state of wudhu when making dua.
3. Sit in tashah-hud position.
4. Raise both hands up to the chest.
5. Praise Allah Ta'ala and recite Durood Shareef before making dua.
6. First ask for forgiveness.
7. Beg Allah Ta'ala from the bottom of your heart.
8. Cry if you can otherwise make like you crying.
9. Recite Durood Shareef again at the end of your dua.
10. End by saying Aameen and wipe your hands over your face.

www.ingramcontent.com/pod-product-compliance
Lightning Source LLC
LaVergne TN
LVHW021053100526
838202LV00083B/5840